I0585520

When Figs Fly

Jane Downing

When Figs Fly

Copyright Jane Downing ©2019

Cover Design: Vivid Covers
Layout & Typset: Close-Up Books

All rights reserved. No part of this book may be reproduced in any form by any electronic or mechanical means including photocopying, recording, or information storage and retrieval without permission in writing from the authors.

ISBN-978-0-6485411-0-3

Published by Close-Up Books
Melbourne, Australia

For Anne and Bevan

Contents

A Block From Home

A block from home the magpies
are busy nest building
The one on the corner has been listening
to politics on the backyard radio
She's a 21st century urban bird
She's worked hard
innovating her real estate

In the crook of the electricity pole
and the electricity wire, she has propped
her pickings, including
twelve similarly wire coat hangers
A plastic fly-swat shoots out
a landing platform
or a flag of convenience

She hovers menacingly
like her house of sticks brethren
Her butcher's beak opening and closing
without song

Local Positioning System

This corner is where the gutter backs up and the road floods.
It is dry now and everyone will forget until it rains again.

Keep going, up past where kittens popped out of the drain once,
summer balls of fur and eyes, in front of the house where the
piano teacher lived;

she said 'you have the hands of a flautist,' so my piano lessons
didn't go far.
This line of trees was lopped around when I was in high school,

see how the branches have been cut to make a canyon for the
power lines to pass through. It's all built up now: No. 32 is on
the spot of the Paddock of One Sheep.

They've put a second storey on No. 29 and the hedge around No.
26 used to seem like something from a fairytale; things are taller
when you are littler.

Turn right at the corner with the apartments. There was a girl
who learned the violin, she lived in the one on the lower left.
Mostly windows are blind eyes but at dusk

she'd put the light on, stage lighting her bowing. Exhibitionist.
Maybe I was smarting from my piano teacher's words, but I see
her ghost in the window every time I pass.

It's a long straight road next. In summer it is the best way to
town because of the plane trees

The temperature drops 10 degrees instantly. And in autumn it rains itchy fluff

with the cockatoos up there ravaging the seed balls. No, that's not a cockatoo.
It's a scrap of paper in the wind.

When Figs Fly

The weight of the heat measures itself against the afternoon light
making them Rupert Bunny languid across cane chairs on the verandah
in the unconvincing shade
It'd better be a record. I don't mind suffering if it's a record
she fans herself with The Age, limp like everything else

His cracker curls into a tube and he puts it back on the plate
G&T? Sun above the yardarm and all that?
They sit there as if some servant will materialize from the mirage of heat
The dog cocks his head on movement up the back
where the pumpkins take shelter under their self-made umbrellas

Orange, lemon, apple, fig – an orchard of sorts against the fence line
rustles as they take off from the shade
A flock of figs she sighs, *look flying figs*
And there they go, hard brown bodies and fidgety wings
I'll get that drink he murmurs as the sparrows resettle

Galah Rain

It's wash day
in an end-of-the-world downpour
They flock dust parched
and make a Chinese laundry
      in grey and pink
on the telephone lines

A circus
of gossip and nitpicking
cambers on the squall
They're silly as wheels
      rotating on the highwire
wings pegged out in the rain

A message
is puffed in feathery morse code
at pauses along the wire
Loquacious in their joy
      they're sharing
their vision to the very last
             drop

Christmas Beetles

On Christmas night the beetles send kamikaze
missions against the French doors
sounding like the opening notes
in a heavy downpour
like the distant artillery fire
of a child's pop
gun

By daylight the massacre pools on the verandah
(the French doors triumphant)
The insects lie motionless on their
backs – turtle still
We sigh over the poor Christmas beetles
(no entomologists amongst us to verify the naming:
they are brown, beetles, that time of year)
Sad, we say,
at a holiday time-of-good-will

No one gets the broom

A peewee finds the larder by midday
skirmishes through the outdoor furniture
comes shopping through Boxing Day
One tough beetle at a time

A Little Ray of Sunbeams

Variations on the Sunbeam frypan recipe for curried rabbit circa 1960

Kill	rabbit in non-toxic trap (do not get myxo-ed up)
Bury	rabbit for one week until the fur pulls off like a glove
Wash	rabbit and soak in salt water bath
Joint	rabbit and talc with flour, salt and pepper
Melt	a little ray of shortening in your Sunbeam
Fry	until golden brown like our wide open plains
Mince	apple and onion and throw into mix
Add	curry (Keens from the jar) and stock (from the pot)
Stir	until thicker thickened thick
Last	add banana and cook all until tender as the night
Eat	with spaghetti and sherry and friends
Stay	rabbit on into the wee hours until the beefs come home

Mummy*

Take me, use me
crush my body and
paint your world with me

Break me limb from limb
to feed your fire
Unwrap me
and expose my canopic guts
Write your life on the rag-paper
of my bindings

Turn my power into powder
a magic potion
a medicinal cure
Macbeth's witches' brew

Why do I expect to be left to rest in peace?

Paint your world with me

* *Egyptian mummies are used for all the purposes listed in the poem, it just feels that way for other mummies*

When the Circus Came to Town

When the circus came to town
our dogs ran away

For three days we imagined them leaping fiery hoops
balancing sure-footed on the tightrope
a tutu perched on their Jack Russell waists

But on Wednesday we smelled them come back
They yapped at the gate begging to come home
'No way you mongrels,' growled Mum
turning the hose on them—
icy retribution for their holiday in the elephant poo

Behind the Big Top they must have writhed in ecstatic abandon
disbelieving their luck
wondrous that the world could be so fine
Until the elephants were loaded up
so the gifts from heaven dried up
and they remembered the comforts of home

Mum used Tina's special apple shampoo (all of it)
and stripped them clean with unforgiving fingers
though elephant poo has a tenacious hold
They did penitence by the wood pile
until they turned their big sorry eyes on Mum
and she finally let them in
To fondle their soft-as-shammy ears up on the sofa

When Mum was cranky (when we were bad)
She'd say

as all Mums do
'Go on then, run away to the circus'

But we never did

Trick Photography

They say these are the days
        you'll remember forever
But you take photos anyway

Then the face in the mirror of the memory
Is not the one in the frame

You are not the little girl
        behind the heat haze of cake and candles
You are behind the garage mortified
        at finding not one minty in the hunt

But you point the camera at your child anyway
        determined to capture a trick of the light
She smiles behind her own singing candles
        And you wonder where the memory hides

A Fortunate Life

Bert Facey's father died before he was two
and his mother abandoned him soon after.
I read his *A Fortunate Life*
propped at the foot-end of my son's hospital bed,
him at the other, top to tail, like we'd slept in the night,
as I wasn't leaving him alone here.

He is pale, and instantly invalided by a pump
attached to a vein on the back of his hand,
saline trickling through the tube,
keeping the vein open in readiness for the biopsy results
that are taking forever to come as Bert arrives
in Western Australia and walks for a hundred and forty miles,
without boots.

He was sent off to work at eight, but my son
hasn't reached that age and the little child opposite
is sobbing as more needles are stabbed into his flesh.
A flimsy curtain hisses around his bed but
I have a soundtrack as Bert is beaten by his employer's son
for hiding the Christmas grog. I see my son
has a Tintin book open though the pages do not turn.
I pretend he's lost in the subtext of the pictures,
or translating the words into Italian.
Bert very nearly did not live.

This time with boots sewn from bags, Bert walks
through the bush, where dingoes howl in the darkest nights.
He is trying to get home which means to his Grandma
who took her grandkids on when she was in her sixties.

A mother outside the room has fallen to the floor, her
waiting for the results over, and she is beating the lino
with her fists as she wails to an unjust god. Grandma
had to sell her home and move to a new colony
and live in dirt-floored huts and take up the
anguish of motherhood again.

Then Bert has another 'mum' – the wife
of his new employer, until she is bitten by a snake
and the dash to a doctor is a daylong ride. It is
interrupted by two doctors arriving, one to sit
on the chair, the other on the bed with us.
'You look comfortable,' says the senior of the two.
My sons face is bright and eager. I sit up. My internal
organs must look nothing like the ones she studied
in her textbooks at Uni.

Much later I read that 'mum's' poisonous snake
was a broody hen roosting at the back of the dunny.
And one day I'll finish reading *A Fortunate Life*
but at the moment we're too busy living our own.

Not Another Hairy Panic Grass Poem*

It was like this: a poet and her son, L-plates plastered front and back, getting up a hundred and twenty logbookable hours. Country road between towns. Favourite band blaring on the radio. *The Panics*. A haze appears up ahead. Across the tarmac, banked on both sides of the road. A mirage shimmering that does not dissolve as they speed toward it. Then they are in the cloud. Ambushed by mini-me tumble weeds. Sliding up the windscreen, caught under the wipers, a bride's train fluting behind. Son screaming. Poet screaming. *The Panics* moaning 'Don't Fight It.' Take the advice. Don't break. Don't swerve. Don't fight it. An eternity then through into the light. What was that, pants the L-plater. That was an experience, says the poet. But she can't write about it. Everyone who has ever stepped wheels into the country -side in December has written a hairy panic grass poem. Sometimes with the same degree of panic as in the car with the poet and her son

tumbling summer haze
with syllables made for this
hairy panic grass

but perhaps the first Hairy Panic Grass Haibun

Wishbones

It turns from scrubbed white to dead-bone yellow on the sill above the sink
A furcula fetched from the chicken's neck for a game as old as the Etruscans

It sits like a water divination rod above the taps, rocks when we touch it
Clippity-clop, rocking-horse-rock on two solid sled-like arms

I will put my pinky round one arm, she'll do the same to the other
Our knuckles will graze, purchase will slip on the smooth old bone

Thumbs will hanker to push against the head that binds the two arms
But our mother says, wait, it won't snap, too young, too flexible

Competition is repressed: we hide our wishes, daughters of the one mother
Maybe it is the same small wish

For now we do not know wishes do not come true, whether we win or not
We do the dishes and watch another Sunday pass, another wishbone appear

Mothers have a rare wisdom: a second chance joins the brittle bone on the sill
Still, how did she ensure we shared the wins?

Vinegar Chips

Vinegar chips
on the beach
salted with sand
burns on finger tips
gullets seared
squabbling like gulls
mine

Burns on shoulders
and nose tips
hats mushrooming
around castles
mother's warnings
forgotten in the hurry
of tide

and time rushing
last chips
hard nuggets
of burnt oil
shake and rattle
in the paper cup
bottom

Vinyl burning
backs of thighs
Not squabbling
to climb up front

Mum's seat empty
all the ride
home

Vinegar on the lips

Patty Papers

Kitchen of antiseptic and cinnamon;
playing with patty papers
            coracles floating on a Laminex lake, one
upturns on the breeze through the screen door:
our sieve straining the garden and the bees

The patty paper dances, waves of white around the edge
like the crinkled tutu of a ballerina
as an engine approaches to din the room
            close and claustrophobic
clunking of chunks of apple
pounding the batter smooth and lickable

Pushing stubby fingers against
            the crackle of paper, moulding, smoothing
into the old patty tin blackened by time not design
They will not sit or fit
They dance and shift
They drown in the lava flow of creamy batter
ready to crust in the heat of the oven on the summer day

Later to peel like a bandaid from flesh
and wad into pellets
Flicked in the bin

A last memory
of a mother's hands
cracking the muffin to find
a nugget of apple in the steam

A last smile
yet unable to eat
chemo tasting the afternoon sour

Noreuil Park

First, there are boots through the carpet of leaves
those crackling noisy symbols of autumn reminding me
of a real carpet – a lurid replica in a grandmother's hallway
(I'm a child tracing the lines and counting the colours)
It's a stumble from sublime to mundane
In one memory lapse

Next, there's the crisp slap of air stinging my cheeks
I'm back at the river watching the fog ride the river downstream
I can't resist the current and travel too – back to that childhood
hallway when the mornings were cold
(central heating was a Soviet plot)
I am searching for slippers, my toes curling up
like the points of Aladdin's boots

Then, the fairy wren is a suggestion of movement
A flash out of the corner of my eye
He is a rare jewel
tiny
turquoise/sapphire/lapis lazuli
twitching amongst the leaves, fifty shades of brown
tail stirring like a stick in a paint pot
He is the pleasure of sitting at my grandmother's dressing table
rummaging amongst powder dusted crystal
squeezing the testicular bags of perfume atomizers
searching for her string of fairy-coloured beads
Saturated in belongingness

Last, the fairy wren takes flight on the warning
of my heavy tread through the autumn drifts

A flash of colour in the river reflected light
Reminder of
nothing but itself: superb

My Grandfather's Clock

The clock in the hall
strikes on the hour
and the half hour
and the quarter and the three quarter
punctuating the night
with memories
of a time before
I could tell the time

When three blind mice
stared down from
above the bed
through the dark and blindfolds
until the jackhammer chirping
of blackbirds
jolted us awake
to the already prickling heat

When an arrowroot
and a fag
were breakfast
for our grandfather
while Nana gave us
a choice of cereal
and milk
left in a can on the backdoor step

When we ate oranges
but only to first see
the writhing snake of skin

spring
after our patience
was stretched
by painstakingly careful knife strokes

And the days stretched
in missing Mum
and dying to tell her
of walks on the jetty
and not falling through the cracks
and jigsaws finished quickly
to clear the table
for tea

In the dark
it could still
be me
waiting for my parents to come back
and take us home
with a new koala
made of real kangaroo skin
to hug

But the threadbare koala
is long since lost
and the oranges
on the tree by the back fence
are now wooden and sour
and the lungs didn't survive
the wake-up ritual
and the scent of funeral lilies
is hardly buried
beneath the smells of age

And the clock strikes
and it's quarter past the hour
but I don't know which

My Guardian Angel

after James Guppy's *The Fairy of Sharp Edges*

Guppy's fairy looks around
a hard glance over her shoulder
directly at you
dark eyes   sleepless gullies underneath each
The skin has a menopausal slackness
but it's a fairy
You can tell by the wings

Guppy's fairy has her back to you
wings akimbo
They're strapped on, the rope digging into the soft flesh
under her armpit
Her wings are not the traditional teardrops of feathers
no, they are black-handled knives   sharp but not gleaming
They have the look of use

Her full bottom lip is adamant
Her mouth will not open to speak
Guppy's fairy does not look happy   to be interrupted
her top lip curls down   not happy at all, exasperated even
her mood like the sound of knives
being sharpened
rasping metal on metal

You are examined in the steely gaze
balanced on a knife edge

Criminal Thoughts

In which I realise I will not make an attractive corpse
In which I carry a broken watch so they'll know the time of my demise
In which I half burn a letter in the grate
In which I leave the curtains wide so I can draw them deep into the night
       against the stalker's prying eyes

In which I plan to wear a wealth of gold so I'll have green bones

In which I file my nails with a look of disdain like a cop show receptionist
In which I practise my identifying-the-loved-one-in-the-mortuary face
In which I make a mistake but that's okay because it is someone else's clue
In which my life of criminal activity bangs me up for another stretch
       between the sheets

In which I flip open my notebook with one hand
       You must understand I have to ask these questions

Coming Home

Having someone wonder where you are when you don't come home at night is a very old human need

Margaret Mead

It is as late as a dead comedian
The last hill is Sisyphean
Margaret Mead was right

He waits on the top step
Moggie playing statues:
Bastet, goddess of Egypt
His bib is moonlight white
his matching paws are poised on the edge
(why isn't he called Socks?)

The cat gets through the door first
populates the dark hallway
mews hello, you're late

we are home

Kyoto

Haiku country
but cannot condense
too much to see

Eating standing
(now called *eating Japanese*)
breakfast at the Kyoto station
the food stranger than the stance

Carp as big as fairytales
displaying their mouths in the moat
Nightingale floors twittering under our feet
Incense burning nostrils within

The camera lens will not encompass height
and breadth and depth
No words to describe
            the thousand word picture
that cannot be taken

Back on the plane
Samurai and *pagoda* and *sayonara*
are shorthand
to soothe the tourist feet
then we're back in a country
where we become lost in the crowd
no longer able to see each other
over the tops of heads

Night Cherry Blossoms At Yoshiwara
after Hiroshige ca 1840

She slips her socked-feet into thongs
because boots are a bugger
and if she's quick, no-one will see

Rubbish bin and recycle bin pulled behind her
are a parade of *taiko* drummers
thundering down the side of the house to the verge

The cherry blossoms on the nature strip
are acting like guests at a wedding
They confetti the grass, the road, her head

She looks down on this soft evening:
the toe-split *tabi* socks
the cheery blossom petals and

the echo of neighbour's bins down the street
Edo, she sighs, *Old Tokyo*
If she's quiet, no one will hear

Keats' Violets

His friend told him about the violets carpeting the graves
This comforted Keats on his deathbed above the Spanish Steps
He already seemed to feel the flowers growing over him

5am jet-lag time lying on a hard bed I can feel the seeds taking hold
in the fragile soil of self, roots pushing through the antecubital veins
and into the eyeballs   to an ache of purification and composting

So I am covered in violets as I walk down into the Roman past
glimpsing the Colosseum, columns of the Forum dead ahead
Clods on my chest heavy in the climb to the room where he died

Petals softly brush the humid air rising off marble
Pollen floats on the drafts of silent sunshine

Sunday Afternoon

Her hair slides are a pair of coracles
on the blue ocean of the sheet
set adrift during lovemaking
released from the storm

There's a block of sunlight over his left thigh
as solid as the rocks along the shore
She wonders the brilliance is not too heavy to stand
but he sleeps not of the dead
(which cannot be peacefully)

Moby-Dick lies abandoned in the shadow of their bodies
dog-eared corners curling like overgrown toenails
He has been reading to her
She has seen a whale domestically in a frilly apron
carrying a sloshing bucket and mop
spring-clean over a ship
His laugh was as athletic as the whale's *spring,*
clean over the ship

The salty smell of sun-shimmered ocean takes her so far away
when she wants to stay here, for when he goes
Somewhere is the low hum of a blowfly giving up on getting out
and running away to sea
She clings to consciousness
feeding on the moment like it's the last
But the wash of sleep is carrying her out

Jacaranda Bloom

The jacaranda is out again
A shatter of colour
against summer green
A reminder of all the things not done
since last year's bloom

Time lost
walking crab-wise
across the year
Wisdom crabbed
with sideways looks
not daring to turn far from the day
to see the day beyond

So now a cloud of jacaranda blue
to hearten the heart
Grips instead at dreams undone

Not Always

Sometimes I forget if I'm in my car or my body
and the light is green
so I go to cross
only someone who *is* in their car
cuts me off
and I graze my leg jumping back onto the pavement

Sometimes I forget if I'm in love or in pain
and his eyes are saying yes
so I come across
and he runs me down
and I forget if this is his body or mine

Sometimes

The Fortune Telling Fish

A Chinese Fortune Telling Fish
is found floating in the pages of the Don Quixote –
caught a decade ago
when reading the book was imperative
until the words swam up around page 782
and the slither of paper fish
was trapped in the snap of the covers closed
keeping its fortune to itself

Placed now on the palm
the fish curls its ruby head
slowly twitches its tail
casually flips
and foretells the obvious

I am fickle

When Sometimes I See Choughs

Sometimes I see choughs
those sociable birds
who hang around in groups
unlike their black-feathered brethren
rooks/ravens/currawongs/crows/
who I also see of course
and wonder   until I am close
are you a poor lost chough?

The choughs swell and ripple across the nature strips
foraging in the rough   with a bit of a swagger
eating ants, caterpillars, also other stough
each individual on invisible elastic that
snaps
back when they stray too far and enough's enough
because they are more family than flock

Flock is for the paper
litter of cockatoos
and blush of galahs
and the deluge of swallows at dusk
not for these compact and neat
identical clones   all except the latest generation
those a tiny bit floughier

They don't fly away
blasé about my tramping feet,
the menace of my shadow
that sends the sparrows fleeing
This gives the illusion of friendliness

or at least tolerant disregard:
grough voices chat only amongst themselves

Sometimes   at these times
I wonder where
we got the word
chuffed
as it describes so perfectly
how I feel when sometimes
I see choughs

Bulrush

Swallows land on the long stalks that
      bend as if they are taking
           the whole weight
                of a pole-vaulter

At a peewee shadow
the flock rise as one
synchronised chaos
reflected   in   the glass of   the pond
Up on the swirls of a ribbon gymnast
Tails like tiny sickle moons
Each a silhouette of a child's broach circa 1950
pinned to the clouds

Drop back
Bulrushes bend
sigh

Welcome

Landscape

<u>Foreground</u>
> geese like slick orange-billed sheep
> grazing across the grass

<u>Background</u>
> a black swan's hook neck gliding
> like a Punch and Judy puppet
> above the line of the river bank

<u>Figure</u>
> a hunched woman, white-haired
> sharp-featured, arid fault lines around
> puckered mouth that has her fingers
> resting on it. Fluty cooing warbling
> whistle. Then quiet; handbag still

<u>Movement</u>
> old man ambles into frame. Called

And Coast

First you have to pass through the trees
At night in the headlights they frame urban
legends of escaped hook-handed criminals
Mist swirls

Then the forest is felled by open sky
but you cannot yet see the beach
Beach houses yes, of wood & outside stairs & verandahs
Up there: the views

But still you have to walk and crunch the grass
watched by a mob of kangaroos so habituated
they just as likely phoned-out for pizza
Walk on by

Finally, sand amongst the moons of marsupial poo
Ahead water inks the picture-perfect sweep
The big moon gilds the peaks and crests
To the horizon

You could stop where the fishermen cast their lines
The cold will bite your ankles, slap you back
You could stop or dredge abrading toes in wet sand
Dive

And coast

Blissters*

1. the dog forcing his face around the screen door in the excitement of you coming home

2. the soft lap of warm sudsy water against a dirty plate

3. a first kiss

4. the cat curling into the shoe box as you try on your new courtly shoes

5. missing the news by ten minutes: ignorance is...

6. the steam rising from the spout of the teapot

7. spooning

8. ice cream

9. the call when you were thinking about him moments before

10. the ingenuity of chopsticks

11. the miracle of gravity

12. turning out the light on a clean kitchen

13. the watermelon smell of fresh cut grass; and the sharp crunch of icy blades underfoot

14. finding a forgotten photograph book-marking a novel while dusting

15. the duck making a perfect landing on its shadow in the moving current

16. the evening scent of jasmine through the open backdoor

17. the last leaf on the elm

*small pockets of joy that sit just under the skin

Contemplating Bliss

Reading Katherine Mansfield makes me languid
I want to recline on a verandah
      to write limpid prose
      and to know my *nerves* far more intimately
      before I dress for dinner

But there is no way to limpidly chop liver
      And no-one to do it for me
Nor any nanny to take *them* away
      I have to send them off to play Lego

So maybe I'll be able to fit in one more story
before the light fades
and his footsteps crunch the gravel in the drive
And maybe in the morning
      when I see the flowering *aloe*
      on the shampoo bottle
I'll feel languid again

City Birds

And the crow was the big black bin bag
and the big black bin bag was the crow
and their blackness shimmered
taking the light to purple

And their struggle separated them, bird and bag
a bridge formed only by a sharp beak
pecking, tearing, woodpeckering
the bloated blackness at his feet

And the incision was a keyhole to the blackness
Snowfalls of paper threaded out; a magician's hankies
Discarded, shaken from the skewering beak
The skin, the fat: to the guts of it

And a smaller bag of viscera found within
cut through and through and through
And the big black bin bag erupts a lava flow of scraps
And low, the happiness of crows

Bonnards' Cat

Pierre Bonnard's White Cat (*Le Chat Blanc*) 1894
has the smug face of a cat and the whipping tail of a cat
and the four legs of a cat, only this is Impressionism: the legs are far too long
Each leg floats like those of a halved octopus not like my cat on the windowsill
But it is like the cat I saw in the movie *The Hurt Locker*
about the war where *we're* bringing democracy to the Middle East
Baghdad, where they need *our* bomb disposal teams   also teams with ca
The streetscape is desolate sand on sand and the cat picks its way
skinny, white fur with a hint of ginger   long   long   legs to clear the rubble

Lilly Pilly

The lilly pilly was there when we came –
trembling
Within, wasps discovered
feasting on virgin white flowers
A shudder of green leaves
as the insect intruders convulsed the native tree

A chill wind blows across the summer –
blooms gone
now the berries
the colour a puzzle:
enigmatic while words tumble
to describe the reds and gold
of the garden's European fall
Are they purple, mauve, or is it magenta?
When darkness spreads across the sky
a blue taints each sphere
They are luminescent in the twilight
the colour of a bruise still new

Clustered, heavy, branches weighted down –
too heavy
The berries fall and are trampled bloody
by the green and gold of the
European trees
that dominate our Australian backyard

The Outscape

Pearl bush glows pale grey
in the moments before the sun
bleaches its soft pink flowers star white
The scorpion, gymnast arched
slips through the crescent door of its hole
the darkness within a smile through the heat of the day
when kangaroos cool their bellies in wallows
and the creek bed bakes into a jigsaw of pottery shards

Haze shimmers the horizon into
an Impressionists painting of itself
beneath a sky that only has its base coat
It's the flat landscape of the outback
where grit rubs you raw
and your carcass will desiccate
          not putrefy

March Heatwave

I've been noticing women's toes. The neighbour's lawn is a badly cooked naan bread. Someone should invent the opposite of a hot water bottle. We no longer have the right to colours. It is reflex to recoil from sour milk. I can't remember his face: I would know it instantly. Silence like the dead air over the radio when the apprentice pushes the wrong button. Toss, tosser, tossest. Caught between reason and raison d'être. At what temperature is nakedness the answer... or is it always a question? I think of myself as a peccable woman. Do-si-do turn to your partner. Turn a cold shoulder, if you only could. Need to find a documented instance of pegs melting on the line. Skin parches under sweat. Mad as a March hare. March as a mad hair. American politics at 3 am must be in the small print of Dante. The smell of rot can rot. Edges are for falling over. Push me. Turn the wine back to water. The Joker laughs, Why so de-lerious? The crow cannot finish his last caw.

Detention Deficit Disorder

How do you write a poem about Manus and Nauru
We've seen the razor wire footage/ listened to the reports
succumbed to Attention Deficit Disorder – look a celebrity died
Will a well chosen image connect
Move someone to action (not me)
like poetry in the old days recited in the heat of revolution
Does this need a personal anecdote
to give it a punch above lecture/harangue
a poignant quote*
A crisis point to bring into focus the human face
that reveals the inhumanity of our country of the Fair Go
turning a willfully blind eye
and blaming the hypocrisy of smiling politicians
Will a reference to Hitler help any (no)
How could the Germans not have known?
It's not as if we don't

History will not be kind
An Apology will be too late
Having written a poem will not have been enough

* *'Poetry is about the grief. Politics is about the grievance.' Robert Frost*

Keep Australia Beautiful

Businessman strides down city street
White shirt and navy tie flying as banner of success

He renames greed—resource management
And exploitation—development

Executive stoops to pick up litter on the corner
Pops it in the bin

Can I be duped into thinking
There is hope

A True History

You know the troopers were sent to catch him
that Ned shot them, one Kennedy unarmed and in surrender
Know when his gasping breath pained their sensibilities too far,
Kelly shot him again as you would a fallen horse—
a dumb sick animal, not the husband of a wife
Under the eye of the laughing jackass Sergeant Kennedy died
and the bullet ricochets still through my breast
ripping out my heart to bleed

But, no, I must and have put out my anger
For it had crowded my heart as tight as a coffin
pushing the love I'd known beyond the border of memory
To love my Kennedy again,
I have had to find a way to forgive his killer
a man who had wrong done to him some say
a man who did great wrong
But just a man

The judge said he apportioned a just punishment
still I understood the weight of the heartache
for those left behind by the hangman's noose.
And yet, my own heart is not so big to understand all from that day:
why I have had to watch as you make him your Hero
The bluff beard, sharp eyes, outlandish armour
were your thousand words to make a star for your legend
while the victims are mute beneath the sod

While I, Bridget Tobin that was
Bridget Kennedy but briefly married
must keen in the small corners you'll allow
Such is the life he left me

Arts Practice

Because windows
are so much like frames
I have to look in
to see how the world
is representing itself today

Nature's Poets

You see them in the countryside
Lone goats staring into the middle distance
collecting details
Sheep fielding life
steady in their gaze
A cow with his own adjective
standing
the thousand word picture of bovine stoicism
ruminating
ultimate
patience

A Drowsing Cat of a Day

It's a drowsing cat of a day
pockets of sunlight are furred with stretched felines
comatose, eyes unblinking
Every step is pushed through honey light
Every thought unfinished

This walk a month ago was all the saddest things in the world
Chinese paper lanterns the morning after the rain
a pregnancy kit abandoned in the laneway by the high school
flowers tied to the lamppost under a handwritten RIP
Every thought caught in the cracks in the pavement

Now there's no more frost
just a lump in the throat
The crows add their disdain in waves till the last note
and the plane trees have knuckles at the end of each branch
Any day soon they'll hit out at spring and burst into leaf

Ode to a Sparrow

To my companion on the upper verandah
I perch here for the bird's-eye-view
You hover for the scraps of human food
Both of us with eyes like the beads on an Edwardian woman's
purse
We're watching, absorbed, intent
The breeze shifting the mugginess of the storm

I want to write about the life below
Peck at the scraps left on the footpath
            a hand held, a dog entwined around a leg, a dribble of
chicken wrap down the hurrying man's chin
You are more honest
You play statues
            garden ornament sparrow impersonations on the rail
It's survival for you
The black feather bib indicates low rank
You are the beggar not the king

I throw you crumbs
And create castles in my own cloudy sky

Confetti

Publishing a book of poetry is like dropping a petal into the Grand Canyon and waiting for the echo

Don Marquis

But we are standing
several metres back
from the canyon's
lip

We must throw
our petals from
here
wishing on a wind
to take them all the way to that
echoing abyss

The air is still
between us
and publication
Not a sigh
as we submit
to what must

Yet isn't it a lovely sight:
All those petals cast up
A confetti of colour
showering
the
landscape

Acknowledgements

The following poems have appeared in the following journals, magazines, or anthologies between 1998 and 2018. Grateful acknowledgement is made to the editors.

'A Block from Home,' *Canberra Times*, Panorama, 19, October 21, 2017.
'A Drowsing Cat of a Day,' *foam:e*, 12, 2015.
'A Fortunate Life,' *Studio*, 74, 18-19, 1999.
'A Little Ray of Sunbeams,' *Quadrant*, 60(6), 94, 2016.
'A True History,' *The Best Australian Poems 2004*, Black Inc., 40-41, 2004; *Quadrant*, XLVII(4), 14, 2003.
'And Coast,' *foam:e*, 15, 2018.
'Arts Practice,' *foam:e*, 12, 2015.
'Blissters,' *Tamba*, 60, 91, 2017.
'Bonnard's Cat,' *Eureka Street*, 23(7), 16 April, 2013.
'Bulrush,' *Social Alternatives*, 37(2), 70, 2018.
'Christmas Beetles,' *Poetry Monash*, 87, 17, 2013.
'City Birds,' *Cordite 52:* Toil, November 2015.
'Coming Home,' *Eureka Street*, 25(13), 13 July, 2015.
'Confetti,' *Poetrix*, 39, 11, 2012.
'Contemplating Bliss,' *dotlit*, 4(1), August 2003.
'Criminal Thoughts,' *Cordite 54:* No Theme V, May, 2016.
'Detention Deficit Disorder,' *Social Alternatives*, 37(2), 70, 2018.
'Fortune Telling Fish,' *Poetry Monash*, 63, 11, 2001.
'Galah Rain,' *Poetrix Selected and New Anthology*, 40, 61, 2013; *Poetrix*, 16, 26, 2001.
'Jacaranda Bloom,' *Centoria* 4, 6, 1998.
'Keats' Violets,' *Windmills*, 13, 17, 2014.

'Keep Australia Beautiful,' *Canberra Times*, Panorama,
    16, October 6, 2001.
'Kyoto,' *Poetrix*, 28, 12, 2007.
'Landscape,' *Rabbit,* The Age Issue, 6, 43, 2012.
'Lilly Pilly,' *Social Alternatives*, 18(1), 70, 1999.
'Local Positioning System,' *Poetry & Place Anthology*, 5-6, 2016.
'March Heatwave,' *foam:e*, 15, 2018.
'Mummy,' *Poetry Monash*, 75, 24, 2007.
'My Grandfather's Clock,' *Spindrift*, 15, 32-33, 1998.
'My Guardian Angel,' *Windmills*, 13, 10, 2014.
'Nature's Poets, *Poetry Monash*, 82, 21, 2011.
'Night Cherry Blossoms at Yoshiwara,'
    Poetry Monash, 89, 6, 2014.
'Noreuil Park,' *Poetrix Selected and
New Anthology*, 40, 2, 2013.
'Not Always,' *Small Packages*, 5, 56, 2002.
'Not Another Hairy Panic Grass Poem,'
    Social Alternatives, 32(1), 43, 2013.
'Ode to a Sparrow,' P*oetry Monash*, 82, 22, 2011.
'Sunday Afternoon,' *Artlook Magazine*, March 2005.
'The Outscape,' *Salt-lick Quarterly*, 2, 44, 2003.
'Trick Photography,' *Centoria*, 11, 32, 2001.
'Vinegar Chips,' *Social Alternatives*, 35(4), 65, 2016.
'When Figs Fly,' *The Best Australian Poems 2015,*
Black Inc., 5, 2015. *foam:e*, 12, 2015.
'When the Circus Came to Town,' *Poetrix*, 20, 21, 2003.
'Wishbones,' *Eureka Street*, 25(13), 13 July, 2015.

www.ingramcontent.com/pod-product-compliance
Lightning Source LLC
Chambersburg PA
CBHW021435110726
47901CB00008B/2436